The Journey To Freedom

Kimberly Cooper

REJOICE
Essential Publishing

Kimberly Cooper/Rejoice Essential Publishing

PO BOX 512

Effingham, SC 29541

www.republishing.org

Unless otherwise indicated, scripture is taken from the King James Version.

The Journey To Freedom/Kimberly Cooper

ISBN-13: 978-1-956775-61-7

LCCN: 2023907612

Dedication

TO ALL OF MY nieces and nephews: I love each of you like my own children. All of you have a piece of my heart. You are our future and I desire that you go further than I. May I be that role model that is encouraging and supportive in your life. May you prosper and successfully accomplish every goal, including God in all of your plans. I'm thankful to have each of you in my life. Remember Philippians 4:13, "I can do all things through Christ who strengthens me". I love yall so much.

Table of Contents

Acknowledgements

I WOULD LIKE TO THANK my Lord and Savior, Jesus Christ. He's first in my life and without Him, I'm nothing. He's been with me every step of the way. I honor Him above all. I want to thank my amazing, loving husband, Ludrick Cooper, for his endless love, support, and encouragement to write this book. Thank you for allowing me the freedom to be and become all God's called me to be, being right by my side. I am grateful we found each other. I'd like to thank my immediate family. My parents, Linda & Freddie, for teaching me morals and standards of life. Without the two of you always loving me, there would be no me. I am an extension of you. To my siblings: Freddie, Teddie(RIP), Lindsey, and Kensey, thanks for believing in your baby sister. I am beyond thankful to have you as my siblings. I love each of you dearly. The clan of 5 we will always be. Thank you to my friends, relatives, and spiritual leaders for believing in me. Your support is appreciated.

INTRODUCTION

I AM THE DAUGHTER OF Freddie & Linda Watkins. I have two brothers (one deceased) and two sisters. I am the baby of the pack. I was born on June 15, 1984, in Florence, SC. I grew up in my hometown Nesmith. The town with no traffic lights or stores. My entire neighborhood was practically like family and community mattered. Growing up, I remember not having much. Coming from a large family, we shared everything, but we always had what we needed. As a child growing up, I spent a lot of my time in church. My mother was ordained to preach while carrying me.

I still recall the little "white church" around the circle from our home. My siblings walked there many days when my mom had to work.

Oh, how I remember St. John Holiness Church, where we were Sister Linda's kids. We had Sunday school, a summary of Sunday school, Testimony service, worship, and preaching. If you were a kid back then, you knew church was a whole 8 hour work shift. Yet that was my family's norm. My mother instilled church and a reverence for God in me at a very young age. I still remember as a little girl riding with the late pastor of the church and mom as they took care of church business as they told me. Looking back now, it seemed like mom was an armor bearer. Even with many life events happening, good or bad, up or down, my mom said to pray and trust God. I still don't know how she did it back then.

As time passed, I became a teenager and now I am an adult woman. Even though I was brought up in church and developed my own relationship with God, I still found myself taking major losses that were taking me away from the promise of God, away from my YES! Since I had a foundation in the Lord, I would depend on His strength to overcome trauma after trauma. For years, God has pressed upon me to share the most painful moments of my life in a book to help others get set free. It took decades for me to walk in total healing and deliverance. You can experience the Lord's peace as I do daily and walk in victory. No matter how far the pain runs, it's not too hard for God to bring true healing to your life.

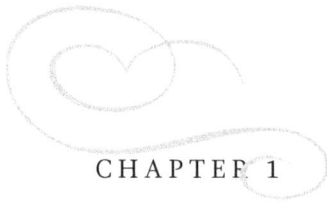

CHAPTER 1

Reflections

GROWING UP WAS QUITE a sheltered life for me. I went to school, church, and work. Once I was old enough at 14, it was the norm. I had no outside interaction unless it was with family or people I saw at school. I still remember not being able to attend the 8th grade prom. I felt ashamed. Mostly all of my classmates went, but it wasn't an option for me. My mom felt engaging in too many secular activities would not be good as a teenager and also, there was the issue of funds to buy a dress along with other items.

As I reflect on my childhood, I just remember not having the peace of mind to have fun and dream at that age. Maturing early in life wasn't a thought for me, but it fell in my lap. I was the go-to person as a child and feeling burdened as a kid was very hard. Internalizing everyone's attitude, emotions, and events led to painful memories. Many have broken down or rebelled as they grew older because they felt like they didn't have a childhood. Some even despise church and turn away from God. It's important to allow children to have fun and for them not to take on adult activities prematurely. The suicide and depression rates are increasing in children, especially those who felt overburdened and misunderstood. A lot of adults have childhood wounds that are unhealed. Some are upset with their parents. God can lift every burden and make up for any loss. He can give you double for trouble (Isaiah 61:7) and bless you mightily so you can live your best days as an adult.

God's hand was on my life then and I appreciate Him. Looking back, I still don't know how I made it out alive without a mental breakdown. The only conclusion would be the Jesus I knew then.

CHAPTER 2

Teenage Woes

GROWING UP AS A "PK" or preacher's kid was really hard. My mother did her absolute best to make sure I knew who God was and why young ladies needed to be seen and not heard. Also, she taught me not to create a bad reputation for myself. At the end of the day, your character is all you got. Once it's flawed, people aren't willing to listen or believe what you say. After all the talks, listening to her preach, and many prayers, I better understood why having a relationship with God was so important. It was so NECESSARY. Even though I didn't grasp it, all I knew was church, prayer, avoiding sin, and holiness were a must.

I remember all I saw was my mom wearing skirts, no makeup, or fancy hairstyles during this time. Although it wasn't a requirement for my sisters and I, it was different for us. My mom was very particular about how we dressed, ensuring we looked like teenagers and not dressing distastefully in revealing clothes. I'm thankful she raised us that way regarding our outward appearance. I still follow those standards. Proverbs 22:6 says, "to train up a child in the way that they should go and when they get old they will not depart from it."

Many children may not understand why their parents may be strict. It's because it's their job to protect them and ensure they are raised in the fear and the admonition of the Lord. Children can be pressured by their peers to be worldly, but they must understand that their parents love them and have their best interests at heart. They may not appreciate their parents' rules right now, but years later, they will learn to as they look around at all the tragedies in the world. My mother's rules and prayers kept me from dying prematurely, not having children out of wedlock, and kept me safe.

Growing up in a small town, you are limited in places you go and things you get to do. The Mall, movies, and major restaurants were an hour away. With having a large family, we didn't travel much. I remember telling myself, "Lord, when I become an adult, I will travel, live, and create many memories as possible, exposing myself to more." I did have small birthday parties with my siblings. My sisters and I shared clothes and our room. I remember, having twin beds and taking turns sleeping with my sisters. Boy, those were the days. We got on each other's nerves. We fussed and fought, then made up as if nothing happened, but that's how we were raised, not to let anything sever our relationship. We were known as the Watkins Girls.

If someone bothered your sibling, you defended and protected them. My siblings will always be near and dear. They are my first set of friends and secret bearers. I love them so much. We are each other's intercessors. My sisters and I realize that we need each other. They are a God-sent. We must appreciate our family while they are here because life is but a vapor (James 4:14). Sibling rivalry isn't good because it caused Cain to kill his brother Abel. Siblings are a blessing. Many children who didn't have siblings wished that they had one. Take time out to bond with yours. If you don't have a brother or sister, God will send people in your life to make up for the siblings that you didn't have growing up.

CHAPTER 3

When Unexpected Death Comes

O N JANUARY 9, 1998, my family received a call saying my brother, Teddie was shot in the head at a pay-phone booth. He was listed in critical condition for the time being to allow my parents to travel time to Biloxi, MS, to sign permission to take him off of life support. My mother was just getting off of an evening shift and my dad had to break the news to her. At 15, I experienced what you see on tv and what no one wants to endure. It was a devastating life event that really hit my family hard.

Prior to my brother being shot, he was actually working at a union based company doing tile in various states all over the US. He was quite talented and found his niche at the young age of 19. He was there working with an uncle, cousin, and other people we knew. My uncle Thomas had to call to deliver the bad news. He was really distraught over the entire event and felt responsible. The truth is that it could have happened anywhere and God knows our expiration date. In 1998, cell phones didn't exist, so payphones were popular. At the time, he was at a phone booth and was shot from behind. My gut tells me he probably knew the person not to put up a fight unless it was a drive-by. Police officers and investigators closed the case with no leads or suspects. My family didn't have the resources to dig deeper, so it remains unsolved.

The comfort my family had was being able to give my brother a proper burial and knowing he did not suffer once the Dr. told my parents he died instantly before hitting the ground. With all remains intact, we were able to have an open casket viewing. Even with our grieving, it still helped to know we could identify him. I still remember visiting H&H Funeral Home, picking out a casket, and making other final decisions with my family. It still seems so unreal. I also took comfort in knowing to be absent from the body is to be present with the Lord (2 Corinthians 5:8).

Months prior, we lost my great grandmother Jessie to cancer. We were still grieving and adjusting. I believe my brother and great grandmother are in heaven with Jesus. My brother's death was a hard blow to my family. I remember still not understanding. It felt like a bad dream. His funeral was at our local middle school. He was a well-known person and with family all over, a larger place was needed. I remember marching in on the day of the funeral and seeing so many people fill the bleachers and the seats of the gymnasium. Who would've thought at 19, he touched so many lives, young and old?

You never know how much of an impact you are making on others. You can't give up doing what God has for you to do. My prayer is that people will love their families and grip them closely. We don't know the minute or hour when our time is up. If you love someone, tell and show them. Give people their flowers while they can enjoy them. Don't take your loved ones for granted. Even with the devastating loss of my brother, I know Teddie felt loved. His last trip home in December was amazing. My family bonded. Teddie, your sweet memories will remain and live on in my heart. July 4th was his birthday. This past year he would've been 40 and for the 1st time, I felt peace.

For that, I thank God. It hasn't been easy, but God gave me strength. Nine months later, my nephew was born. Even in what seems sad and depressing, joy and happiness were born on October 13, 1998.

Isaiah 66:9 says, "I will birth something new from pain." I am persuaded that God can help us even in low dark places. God gave me this prophetic message through this scripture to encourage me. Prophecy edifies, comforts, and exhorts (1 Corinthians 14:3). God's words have given me tremendous hope throughout the years through my nephew's birth. He gave us beauty for ashes (Isaiah 61:3). During the darkest moments of losing my brother and great grandmother, God gave us strength and comfort. He took all the worry and unbearable pain away. He is with us in the good and bad times. He will never leave us nor forsake us (Hebrews 13:5).

CHAPTER 4

Life After Loss

FOLLOWING MY BROTHER'S DEATH is when things really went downhill for me. After 20+ years of marriage, my parents decided to call it quits, ending in divorce. Leading up to the divorce, I saw things in my home that no child should endure. Two people that once said, "I love you," were closing the chapter. The enemy loves to destroy marriages and we must fight for our marriages and honor our vows before the Lord. Divorce is traumatic for children and causes dysfunction even into adulthood. God can break the generational curses of divorce. If undealt with, marriages will be broken and destroyed from one generation to the next.

During that time for me in grade school, kids got picked on for being raised in a single parent home. It wasn't cool and it seemed like it was the latest gossip. So many kids have ended their lives prematurely because of bullying. We must cover our children in prayer and declare that if a man's ways pleases the Lord, God will keep his enemies at peace with him (Proverbs 16:7).

I was so unhappy about my parents' marriage dissolving. I wanted my parents' marriage to work, but even as a kid looking back, there were things I didn't understand. I could see that they weren't happy. The grief of my brother's passing took a toll on my parents' marriage. Husbands and wives must give each other time to grieve and be there for one another. Losing a child is hard because they are a part of you. God can divorce-proof your marriage and help husbands and wives bond again.

Once my parents divorced, my mother was an official single parent, raising kids, paying a mortgage, making ends meet, and still dealing with the loss of my brother. Every few days, my mom went by Teddie's grave. Seeing her struggle and knowing my family took a large blow were feelings I can't describe. I still was in shock and denial as life was still happening. I recall my mom saying that Teddie came to her in a dream because she wasn't giving him up and he was chasing her, pulling her to come with him. She begged, "No, I'm not ready. Let me go then!" I don't know if it was fear or what, but I saw my mom deal with so much concerning his death. She only visited his grave on his birthday, holidays, or to clean alongside his grave and add more flowers.

Although I don't have children, I can't imagine the pain of unanswered questions. No mother wants to bury their child. Through it all, God is close to the broken hearted and binds up their wounds (Psalm 34:18). No pain is too deep for God to heal. God can deliver us from fear and any torment from the enemy. Although my parents divorced, years later, my relationship with my dad was restored and healed. My parents now have a healthy relationship as friends.

CHAPTER 5

Losing Our Glue

AS PREVIOUSLY MENTIONED, MY great grandmother died 6 months prior to my brother's murder. Here I was processing these feelings of sorrow, sadness, and unbelief. Cervical Cancer is what killed her. I questioned how it wasn't caught in a time when all I ever knew was her going to the Dr. and having her white bags of medicine afterwards. Jessie Lorine Skinner was her name. I remember my family and I took her to Huntington Beach, where she wanted to go. It was her last wish while in Hospice care. I'm happy that my family could pull it off with no issues lol!!

On that day, it was sunny, peaceful, and just a great family outing celebrating the glue of our family, giving her the flowers she deserves as I believe in so dearly. Grandma seemed so chill, laid back, and very much at ease. I knew she was a woman of faith. Even prior to her terminal illness, she believed in God until the end. I miss her so much. I can remember times when she was the one that supported my mother, my siblings and my welfare. When mom didn't have a babysitter while working graveyard shifts, my great grandmother was the go-to. It never failed. She made sure we were fed and bathed before we went home to relieve our mother.

Writing this alone brings tears to my eyes because I realize Grandma was our only hope besides God at the time. With little family support and things becoming dysfunctional, she really helped make sense of things. I still remember her coming to church with my family and I and testifying about her faith even in trying times. Grandma loved all five of us no matter what. She raised my mother as her own daughter. With my mom in ministry, she would support her even if others didn't. I always heard her tell my mom to pray and keep her hands in God's hands. Leading up to her last day, I had to ride the bus over to her house and sit with her. Everyone took turns until her last breath. I'm glad I had the chance to spend time with her in her final moments, but most importantly, to love on her as I knew she loved me.

"Chelle" as she called me, I can still hear her sweet soft voice calling me. Her beautiful silver hair and blue/grayish eyes are all I knew. She had a heart for wanting our family to make it. My great grandmother left us a legacy and provided an example of faith. She truly fought a good fight a faith. She could have complained many times during her doctor's visits, but her faith in the Lord gave her joy and strength. The joy of the Lord is our strength (Nehemiah 8:10). It's important to get regular checkups from the doctor to make sure we are in great health. God gives us wisdom and by His glory, medical technology has evolved so that people no longer have to die from diseases that were prevalent decades ago. May you prosper and be in good health even as your soul prospers.

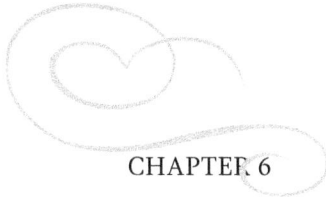

CHAPTER 6

Running Away

*A*TTENDING HIGH SCHOOL WAS such a blur. Instead of enjoying and living the care free life, I was really masking the pain. I made really good grades, dressed well, my hair always slayed, but I was broken! All I could think of was running away and crawling underneath a rock. With God, we don't have to pretend, but we can have total healing.

I wanted to run away from my family and things that reminded me of how I was the girl from a broken home. I did not have a good relationship with my parents at this time. I disliked the fact that I worked my entire high school journey, not having any fun. I had to buy my school clothes, senior supplies, senior trip, prom, and anything else I needed. I thank the Lord for an aunt by marriage that allowed me to live with her and treated me as her own daughter. That was a blessing to be able to get some bonding time and be able to experience some travel and normalcy for a change. Having someone to make time, listen, and ensuring you are okay makes a difference in a girl's life. God will send people into our lives at the right time.

We must trust His plan and be open to the people He wants to remove from our lives. In the end, there still was something more I craved. I took the Armed Services Vocational Aptitude Battery (ASVAB) test in my junior year just to get out of class. By my senior year, I enlisted in the US Army delayed entry level program. Prior to that, I had plans to attend college. That all went out the window for the opportunity to get away from all the madness and anger I harbored on the inside. Graduation Day came and I graduated with honors receiving a life scholarship. My dad wasn't there and my mother left early for whatever reason. I was really disappointed. By that time I had given up on family life. It didn't seem important. All I needed was to feel loved, supported, and like I really mattered.

On July 3, 2002, I left for boot camp. I purposely left a day before Teddie's birthday to avoid feeling grief or seeing my family sad. Looking back on things now, I probably didn't need to enlist because it was never God's plan. Education was always important to me. I had high hopes for myself and being successful. The military was a getaway and quick fix. Boy was I wrong! I was in basic training breaking down. The only 2 people that came to Military Entrance Processing Station (MEPS) were my older sister and my dad to see me off. It was another disappointment in the books.

Men may make their plans but it is the Lord who will order their steps (Proverbs 16:9). We can't run from our problems because they will be unresolved and keep resurfacing again. Since I was internalizing everything from childhood until that moment in basic training, I had an emotional breakdown when it was time to handle my weapon. It wasn't anything with my behavior or acting irresponsibly. I just couldn't see myself using a gun that took my brother's life. It hit me like a ton of bricks. What on earth was I doing in the US Army?

I can't be a part of something that could potentially take lives. Flashbacks of my brother's death came rushing to me. The thoughts and emotions I felt in 1998 when we got the call that rocked my family's lives forever resurfaced. There was no way I could stay in the Military. So naturally, my platoon leaders and other recruits at the time were nice and sympathetic. I cried and explained what had happened. As they tried to build my confidence, I flat-out told them, "No I Can't Do This!" I felt ashamed and disappointed with myself at the same time. I was out-processed and went home. I felt defeated and upset for not having the mindset to push beyond my feelings.

So many people are battling mental health issues but God can deliver us. Many are the afflictions of the righteous but God delivers us out of them all (Psalm 34:19). After returning from basic training, I decided to enroll in college in an attempt to be productive and achieve my goals. Still, I was not getting that I needed to face my root issues and I was just not focused. In 3 semesters, I managed to forfeit my life scholarship. Dropping classes, failing grades, and not being disciplined enough all contributed to this. I had no real relationship with God, still philandering through life, and no real identity of who I was and all I possessed. This time was such a hard season of my life. Everything seemed to be going wrong in my life and I felt like I couldn't catch a break. All I felt was failure, guilt, shame, and defeat!

Many are going through life just as I was. Empty, depressed, lost, and broken while not wanting to deal with the real problem. They are trying to keep busy with work or other activities while hurting deep inside. Cry out to God and surrender all to Him. Deep is calling upon the deep and through God, we can face our giants and mountains. Every Goliath in your life will fall. Your healing is on the way. God will order your steps and reveal His purpose for your life.

CHAPTER 7

A Time To Face The Music

I REMEMBER FACING DEPRES-SION, GUILT, shame, family dysfunction, and the grief of losing my brother. In the multitude of counselors, there is safety (Proverbs 11:14). Many don't believe in counselors but know that God has anointed trained professionals who can help them get free. I found a therapist that offered (CBT) Cognitive behavior therapy, basically talk therapy. Finally, I have a licensed professional to express my thoughts and emotions to who would help me make sense of all of my inner issues, even the daddy issues from being abandoned as a kid. For the first time, I felt free in a safe environment to put my deepest feelings into words. No judgements, backlashes, or worries at this point. Even with getting therapy, this went against everything I was taught and what my family believed. At the end of the day, it didn't matter. I needed to do this for myself and get the help I needed to be whole in every aspect that God intended.

Growing up in church, I still recall hearing depression wasn't for Christians. Depression isn't what God desires, but DEPRESSION is Real! Because of this teaching, many pastors have committed suicide because they didn't use all the available resources. My family had this saying, "What goes on in this house stays in this house." Sharing with some family members that I received counseling was a disappointment. They seemed to speak against or brush me off about it. Talking to a professional therapist was the best thing I ever did. It gave me freedom and liberty. I'm not ashamed. I'm a huge advocate for mental awareness. Be whole in your mind, body, and soul. After so much toxicity and unhealthy relationships, I was finally going in the right direction of really loving myself. I decided it was time to start fresh and wipe the slate clean. For once, this was all for the right intention and not for running away. People may not understand your journey to recovery, but you have to do what's best for you. It's better to be sound mentally than to be in a mental institution or a casket. We have to get delivered from people. Even though they may love us, they don't always understand what's needed for your deliverance. Don't listen to the opinions of man but be led by God's Spirit. Because of counseling, I'm in a much better place today and God gets all the glory.

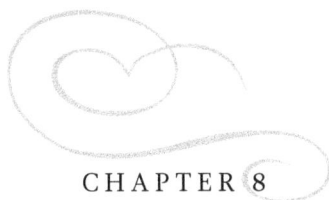

CHAPTER 8

Relocation

O n August 25, 2013, I received an invitation to go stay with PJ and his wife Lillian. PJ was family and like a father figure to me. He knew I had gone through such a hard time and needed to hit the RESTART button. I was really excited and thankful for the opportunity he and his wife was allowing me. Of course, I accepted. So I packed, said my goodbyes, and was on the road to the Midwest in Madison, WI. Upon arrival, I realized the weather and culture were completely opposite from what I was used to. That didn't stop me. I was determined to create a better life of happiness for myself.

After two weeks of living in Wisconsin, something traumatic happened to me. PJ offered sexual suggestions to me. I couldn't believe it. We were in the tv room one evening after watching a movie. I was about to exit to go to my room for the evening when he began to make sexual conversation. He suggested we could be in a romantic relationship and I could live there continuously. I was in shock to the point of freezing up as I sat there, scared out of my mind. He proceeded to turn on a porn DVD. He asked me personal things about my body. I was so humiliated as if he had planned this all along. This was blood and I always looked to him as a father when my dad wasn't in the picture. I kept going back and forth in my mind to break and run, but I was too afraid.

By this point, I didn't know what PJ was capable of. He then proceeded to unbutton his pants, asking me to do the same. I begged and pleaded with my hands raised in the air to please stop and don't do this to me. I told him this was inappropriate and I wasn't interested in having a relationship with my own family. After much small talk, he finally backed down. I left the room as fast as I could. I was scared, terrified, and not knowing if he would rape me. He didn't follow me into the guest bedroom, which was a good thing. I quickly called my girlfriend in South Carolina. It was really late by that time with an hour difference. She knew immediately something was wrong. I cried as I explained to her. I dreaded the thought of telling my mother, as PJ and she were very close.

The next morning I managed to tell my mom. She cried and begged me to come home, fearing for my well-being. I'm sure all those feelings of a mother that lost a child came rushing back to her. My mother and I talked for a long time as I expressed that I wouldn't allow this situation to make me move back home to South Carolina. I was so scared but I knew I needed this move to really be in a different place in my life. I did promise to come home if things got bad. I wanted to buy time to put together a plan to get my own place. This was one of the hardest places I'd been in. By the Grace of God, I made it. I was sleeping with a knife under my pillow.

The enemy is crafty and always is looking for a way in. He is roaming around like a lion, ready to devour us (1 Peter 5:8). We must be prayed up and full of God's Word to resist temptation. We must flee from evil at all costs. Joseph fled from Potiphar's wife when she kept pressuring him for sex (Genesis 39). He left his coat in her hands. He knew it was better for her to have it than for him to fall into temptation. God kept me safe from the enemy.

Luckily, I had a job to get me out of the house in the daytime. When I got home, he was controlling, narcissistic, and bullying, trying to get me to fold. Thankfully, he introduced me to a neighbor of his who indeed was a ram in the bush from God. Tracy was indeed the Ram God used. Upon meeting and speaking to her a few times, I felt I could confide in her. I was desperate, to say the least. I didn't care and I knew I had to tell someone in case something happened to me. Many are afraid to open up. Don't let shame prevent you from getting help. God doesn't condemn us or shame us. His love covers a multitude of sins (1 Peter 4:8).

After expressing to Tracy what happened, she showed me so much love, compassion, and sympathy. With her being much older, it was like having an older sister to look out for me. She let me know I had a place to stay. By this point, I could hug and kiss her. A complete stranger took me in after a traumatic experience. I quickly learned from some investigation of my own, PJ was a registered sex offender. Who would've ever thought? Certainly not my family back in the Carolinas or my mom, for that matter. Otherwise, she'd forbid my move from the jump. As time went on, it really got challenging to live with PJ. He was really ticked off that I didn't give in.

One morning while on the phone was when it came to a head. He demanded that I hang up with my mom and I told him NO. He grew angry and said, "I can leave if I can't play by his rules. I don't care if it is Jesus Christ on the phone." I didn't know if my mom could hear him cursing and yelling at me in the background, but I didn't want her to worry. I quickly told her bye. PJ told me I had to leave and be gone before he came back home. I never packed so fast in my life. I called Tracy quickly as she was my neighbor down the condo plex. Without hesitation or reneging, she brought over her spare key, which was history living with PJ. Without any apologies from him, I moved on and didn't look back.

Tracy was the ram in the bush that God had for me. From that moment on, she became my family, more like a sister. God's grace and mercy covered me. Moving in with Tracy gave me the most peace I had in a very long time. I still was scared that I would see him living in the same unit. Jesus shielded me. Not one day in the months I stayed with Tracy had I seen him. It was a blessing indeed to have met my new friend. I was so ashamed that I had to deal with that and had to tell someone else. I knew God's hand was in it because, at that moment, I realized Tracy and I both were going through life changes and God wanted us to be there for each other.

There were no limits to my stay but I didn't want to overstay my welcome. I landed a great job and was able to save and get an apartment. I thank God each day for keeping me during that traumatic event. The rude awakening began when I moved into my own place. I was having nightmares of someone being in my apartment.

I was afraid to meet people and even go out to do things. Even while walking in public, I'd panic if people walked too close or seemed to follow me. PJ did a number on me. I kept thinking, "What did I do? I wasn't dressed inappropriately; I wasn't talking in explicit language. What made him think it was okay?"

All of those questions plagued my mind daily. Even with wanting to date after that, it was hard as I had trust issues. How could blood betray you? No excuses could satisfy how it left me feeling. If you are going through with what I've dealt with, don't blame yourself. PJ needed deliverance and what happened to me wasn't my fault. Demons were influencing his decisions to assault me sexually. Eventually, after deep thought, I found a therapist. That's when I found out I had PTSD. I thought only military veterans experienced such things. I was learning the effects traumatic events have on people. I'm glad I wasn't ashamed to seek professional counseling. I will never forget my therapist in Wisconsin calling me a survivor. With several sessions, I was able to cope better.

CHAPTER 9

Getting Back to God

I AM IN MY 30s and have grown up in church all my life. I believed in the God my mother told me about, and heard testimonies about. I prayed, cried, and paid tithes and offerings, all based on my mother's relationship. Not that I doubted Him, but I realized I needed my own personal relationship with Him more now than ever. I remember, as a kid going down to the river and being baptized all for the sake of my mom. She wanted my sisters and me to get baptized, so we did. I knew deep down it wasn't for the right reasons, but I really didn't have a choice. God wants all of your heart, not some of it. Make Jesus the Lord of your life and ask Him to reign in your heart.

You will not be disappointed. It's important to have the right motives. God knows what's in our hearts and will draw us closer to Him.

Fast forward to this time, God tugged at my heart more to create a relationship with Him and for my sake. Not riding on the coat tail of what I was taught or believed as a kid, it was time for me to do this for myself. Getting baptized again as a true born believer was the best decision I ever made. I still remember going down in that chilly water and when I came up, I praised God! I spoke in tongues. The Holy Ghost came upon me. I've never felt that before. It was a Tuesday night at corporate prayer. Two ladies prayed with me for my breakthrough. On that night, God met me fair and square. For the 1st time, I did something that was a big deal. I gave God a Yes!

CHAPTER 10

When
Depression
Comes

WHAT IS DEPRESSION? AC-
CORDING to American Psychi-
atric Association, Depression
(Major Depressive Disorder) is a common and
serious medical illness that negatively affects
how you feel, think, and act. Depression causes
feelings of sadness and loss of interest in activities once enjoyed. It can lead to different emotional and physical problems that decrease your
ability to function. For many years, as I can recall, I've dealt with that ugly thing called DE-
PRESSION!! So there I said it.

In my teenage years, I experienced symptoms but didn't have the proper care or treatment to cope. I still remember telling my mother that I was depressed. Back then, people didn't speak about mental illnesses or educate themselves; instead, they said it was the devil. Yet there was no remedy or solution given to what I felt. I suffered in silence to what spilled over into my adult life. Then, I experienced many symptoms: from being super bubbly and having a zest for life to being withdrawn and beat down. Through it all, God never left me. I still had the ability to think to seek help. James 5:16 says to confess your sins to one another and you will be healed. It's better to tell someone what you are going through than to hold it all in.

On many occasions, I saw a therapist for Cognitive Behavior Therapy (CBT). I will tell anyone that experiences depression or anxiety to see a certified therapist. It works! Seeing a counselor literally saved my life. Having someone to talk things out to became a human diary when I felt I had no one to open up to with the capacity to give me sound advice. Depression wanted to suck the life out of me. There were times I lost my appetite and lost weight. I cried on many days, asking God, "Why me?" It felt like my very core was being ripped from me. So many times, I thought I would lose my mind.

Even in my darkest moments, I remember finding this scripture in Romans 8:38-39. And I am convinced that nothing can ever separate us from God's love. Neither death nor life, neither angels nor demons, neither our fears for today nor our worries about tomorrow, not even the powers of hell can separate us from God's love. No power in the sky above or in the earth below indeed, nothing in all creation will ever be able to separate us from the love of God that is revealed in Christ Jesus our Lord.

That scripture spoke to me and ministered to my soul. Come hell or high water, I'm staying with God. I'm never letting go of His hand. God's love lifted the heavy burdens that I had been carrying. To this day, I am an advocate for mental health. It's very important to not just be physically healthy, but one must be healthy emotionally as well. Don't allow your emotions to dictate your day. Or the devil will try to fight you from getting the help that you need. The enemy will speak through people to stop you from experiencing freedom. Remember, Satan spoke through Apostle Peter and Jesus had to rebuke him (Matthew 16:23).

Depression can hold you up from walking into your God-given purpose in life. It leaves you stagnant, where you don't have the drive or ambition to go after your dreams. In the midst of depression, I felt so alone and abandoned. I remember hearing different family members and people claiming to love me speak negatively about people with mental illnesses. It saddens me that some aren't educated enough to know that depression isn't something that you inflict upon yourself. Some causes may be Winter blues, Hormonal imbalances, and traumatic events just to name a few. That was when someone pointed me to Psalm 27:10, When my Father and my mother forsake me then the Lord will take me in. This is another scripture that I replay in my mind. God always came through and gave me what I needed. He always sent people along to remind me of His love and strengthen my faith in Him even more.

As scripture tells us in Psalm 30:5, weeping may endure for a night, but joy cometh in the morning. In spite of everything I have been through, I still tell God thank you. There's no place I would rather be than living in the fullness of God. My greatest joys and victories were with God. My Daddy made me stronger and I was able to love all of me. With much consistent prayer, getting in my Bible like my life depends on it, I learned what you feed your mind and soul will eventually come out. I started fasting to die to myself and putting me first. It's okay to say Yes to me and No to others. No one can pour from an empty cup. After the initial filling, one must go back for refills often. Being a Christian with a therapist is one of the healthiest things I've done. By the grace of God, I'm free. I will remain faithful in my walk with God and maintain my mental health.

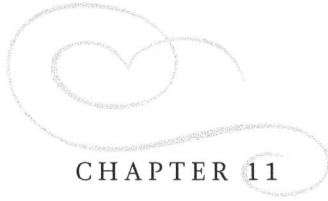

CHAPTER 11

Overcoming

E ARE OVERCOMERS THROUGH Jesus Christ. He was God in the flesh and He showed us how we could overcome through Him (John 1). He is our high priest and understands what we are going through, yet without sin (Hebrews 4:15). Through Christ, we can get victory over every situation. I knew it was more work to be done on my journey of being a Christian. Living for God was way cooler versus living in sin. I just had to face the root causes of my problems. At that moment, I decided to make it my business to develop a closer walk with God. After all, depression, feelings of guilt, hurt, shame, defeat, rejection, and generational curses would bury me alive. I refused to continue the cycle of what others had gone through in my family or the issues I inflicted upon myself. I needed a better way. God was my answer to all of my questions. Come Hell or high water, I'm not letting go.

For many years I felt a void and sometimes like an orphan even with living parents. God's love gripped me and I remember reading (Psalm 27:10)- My Father and mother may abandon me, but the Lord will take care of me. The reality was that my own family wounded me with much betrayal, dysfunction, toxicity, and sabotage. I was angry and bitter. I wanted to write them all off. I struggled with the past offenses over and over again in my mind. I had no peace and it literally crippled me.

My heart was always open as I deeply love my family. I consider myself to be a loyal person and I'm there for my loved ones. Love always wins!

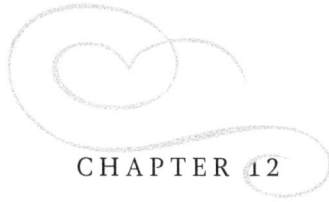

CHAPTER 12

Maintenance

*E*VERYONE KNOWS IN ORDER for a vehicle to properly function, it requires keeping up all major components. If you want reliable transportation, you must put the work in to reach your destination. One must pray daily. Prayer is the most important conversation you have on any day: from the time you hit the floor, periodically throughout the day, and ending your evening in prayer. We must pray over our day before starting it, giving thanks for getting through it, and for protection as we sleep.

Having prayer with God is an actual two way conversation. We must wait for our answer. In order to hear God, we must be clear, focused, and also open to receive. Release what's in your heart to God. He will heal, console, comfort, and keep us. His direction and answers will be made plain as day if we listen and pay attention. Some things won't come with prayer alone, but by fasting and sacrificing, such as devoting time to God and seeking His presence. Galatians 6:9 says, "And let us not be weary in well doing: for in due season we shall reap, if we faint not." If we pray, fast, and faint not, we will overcome and get the victory as the Word tells us.

Creating a peaceful atmosphere in our homes and our relationships, and meditating on God's word is necessary. Joshua 1:8 reads, "This book of the law shall not depart out of thy mouth; but thou shalt meditate therein day and night, that thou mayest observe to do according to all that is written therein: for then thou shall make thy way prosperous, and then thou shalt have good success." No one backslides overnight. It's usually because they were not maintaining their spiritual temple. They stop reading their Bible, praying, and fasting. Instead of spending time with God, they started replacing God's time with worldly things such as secular TV and secular music. The priests in the Bible were ordered to keep the fire burning on the altar once God set the offering ablaze (Leviticus 6:12). We are mandated to keep the fire of God burning within us. We must fan the flames (2 Timothy 1:6) and never allow the flames of the Holy Spirit to dwindle.

CHAPTER 13

Get a Mentor

As I looked up the word Mentor in Merriam-Webster, it means a trusted counselor, guide, someone who teaches or gives help and advice to a less experienced person. A mentor is something I desperately needed, not someone secular, telling me things off the top of their head. In the Spirit, everyone needs a mentor, a God connection that holds the keys to unlock or activate your God-given gifts. In growing and going through this thing called life, I realized that I wasn't going to get all I needed in church. If you want to reach your potential and live in purpose, you must choose a mentor that has the capacity to assist as a midwife to help you give birth. Discernment is vital in choosing a mentor, otherwise your mission can be aborted.

I'm so grateful to my Apostle spiritual covering, Cierra L. Jones my midwife. I got back up and decided to live my truth. Throughout the Bible, we can see the importance of a mentor. Naomi mentored Ruth. Jesus mentored the disciples. Apostle Paul mentored Timothy. It's a blessing to have a mentor because we can pull on their wisdom and learn from their mistakes. They have experienced things that we haven't yet and we can glean from them. God will send you a mentor if you ask Him and they will help you get to the next level in Him.

CHAPTER 14

Affirm Yourself Daily

NOWING WHO YOU ARE is very important, especially for me. Affirming myself every day is like a daily vitamin. Replace negative thoughts with positive words to influence the mind. Replace bad behaviors with good behavior. Affirmations can change your entire view of your life by causing you to be better, do more, and live a fulfilling life. Reciting and writing affirmations down each day can really make a difference in your inner soul. Life and death lies in the power of the tongue (Proverbs 18:21). We must speak words that are edifying to the hearer (Ephesians 4:29). We must pray that we see ourselves the way God sees us. If we don't believe in the vision that God gives us then others won't as well. God didn't make a mistake when He called us for the assignment. We are God's workmanship and His handiwork (Ephesians 2:10). We can do all things through Christ who strengthens us (Philippians 4:13). We are more than a conqueror through Jesus Christ (Romans 8:37).

CHAPTER 15

New Beginnings

*A*FTER OVER 10 YEARS of being divorced, God allowed me to remarry again. I Married the love of my life, Ludrick N. Cooper. Finally I am with someone that believes in God and puts Him first. He truly loves me. Honestly, I didn't see marriage in the cards after many painful relationships. After so many toxic relationships, you question something real. Once I met my now husband, I realized that God had someone just for me. When someone loves you, it doesn't hurt. They add rather than take from you. I thank God every day for my husband. I'm grateful to God for sending someone I could grow with. My husband doesn't hinder me from pleasing God, but he wants to live as a kingdom couple.

The blessing of the Lord makes you rich and adds no sorrow (Proverbs 10:22). God doesn't get the glory out of bad marriages. He will not give you someone who is mean and beats on you. Remember, love is patience and kind. It doesn't easily boast or holds records of wrong doings (1 Corinthians 13:4-8). God has a rib (wife) for every man. God has mandated that a husband will leave his father and mother and be cleaved unto his wife and the two shall become one flesh (Ephesians 5:31). God will make sure that your husband will love you as Christ loves the church (Ephesians 5:25). It's taken me from the fear of failing and being disciplined to now stepping out on faith to do what my passion is and fulfill my purpose on earth. Serving others is a gift from God. To embrace, empower, and pray for others is what I've been called to do. The feelings of being stuck went away. I am no longer a prisoner to myself. There's power in using your words, the power of freedom and liberty. Oh, what a breakthrough this has been for me.

I will continue to use my voice to help others that may feel lost or ashamed. The process wasn't easy, but well worth it. I will stay in line

to reach the Promised Land. Only God made all of this possible. He gave me the strength to press and run on. Circumstances came up, but they did not define me. That's when God allowed me to rewrite my story. My Heavenly Father is the author and finisher of my faith. Getting back to my yes is the best thing I have ever done.

CHAPTER 16

Forgiveness

THE POWER OF FORGIVENESS is important along your journey of wholeness. It was so hard at times to forgive people who hurt and wronged me. Once I really began to walk with God and truly opened my heart, I gave Him those burdens. Today I stand with a heart of forgiveness and love. Walking in unforgiveness can derail your future. God will impart and give you access to amazing people and places if you forgive. Our behaviors show a mere reflection of our heart. Only when you forgive, will you feel so much lighter. God commands us to forgive those who wrong us. I understand that it can be a difficult task to forgive others that hurt or offend us, but when we ask our Heavenly Father and truly mean it,

Christ will give us strength to overcome feelings of anger and bitterness.

When I learned to give my issues over to God and leave them there, I saw Him move on my behalf. God loves us and wants to help us. Ephesians 4:31-32 reads, "Get rid of all bitterness, rage, and anger, brawling and slander, along with every form of malice. Be kind to one another, tenderhearted, forgiving one another, as God in Christ forgave you." Through His grace, we can receive divine help to do things that we couldn't do in our own strength.

The journey to forgiveness can be long and painful. Just when you think you've healed and over it, something triggers you. My process of walking in forgiveness was to be the first partaker. I had to accept and acknowledge what happened, showing compassion for myself. This time I needed to extend grace to myself. When processing trauma and painful memories, one would need a strong support system. I recall many couch sessions to see my therapist. As Christians, we've got to kill the stigma of saying a person is weak or someone has lost faith. After all, we must use discernment and wisdom in dealing with our mental and spiritual well-being. To be whole, one must be healthy emotionally, mentally, physically, financially, and spiritually. It all comes together full circle and you have to do the work.

I began to really experience forgiveness when I started praying and seeking God about the true matters of my heart. I no longer wanted to hold on to the residue and remnants of the past. I remember asking God to expose the hidden things that I suppressed and recall them back to my memory. It was a painful, yet freeing experience. Once and for all, it was time to let it go! Carrying unforgiveness is a huge price and penalty to pay. If I had held on to it, health issues could have happened and I'd be delayed in life and also bleeding on others, which was the reality of my life at the time. The idea of living and not coming into the fullness of who God called me to be, scared me. Forgiveness is a change of mind and heart posture. It's a choice and I'm walking all the way in the freedom of forgiveness.

Forgiveness frees us. And because Jesus forgave me, I am called to forgive others. Matthew 6:14-15 says, "For if you forgive others their trespasses, your heavenly Father will also forgive you, but if you do not forgive others their trespasses, neither will your Father forgive your trespasses." This commandment was made by our Lord and Saviour. Forgiveness relieved me from feeling like I was always carrying a ton of bricks on my heart and shoulders. When you have a connection to the source, I'm a living witness, you will forgive and do things that in your human flesh would seem impossible. Philippians 4:13 says, "I can do all things through Christ who strengthens me". I forgave them all.

Remember, forgiveness is for you, not for the offender because usually the person you are mad at has moved on with their life while you are stuck reliving the pain. Let it go. Trust God. Remember, the disciples asked Jesus how many times they have to forgive and He said seventy times seven (Matthew 18:22). As we forgive, our Heavenly Father will forgive us of our sins (Matthew 6:14).

CHAPTER 17

Embracing All of Me

FOR SO MANY YEARS, I've lived in the shadow and background of others. I have doubted my very existence and purpose here on earth. Me being the baby of 5 made it extremely hard to have a voice. I felt powerless and invisible. I'd asked God often, "Why did you choose this family for me that won't even hear me out?" All the while, I made an agreement with God to come here to earth. I always felt like the stepchild and black sheep of the family because I always went the opposite of others. To constantly hear you're not experienced enough, or you don't know what you're talking about began to shape my world. Early on as a child, I always heard, "You're such an old soul." I always found myself giving adults advice. It felt good because, talking with peers, I felt like a total oddball.

I began to accept that I was different and God had marked me for His special plan. As I interacted and connected with like-minded people, it all came together. According to Proverbs 27:17, Iron sharpeneth iron, so a man sharpeneth the countenance of his friend. I'm so thankful for my Divine covenant connections. It's been amazing with some growing pains when I found out truly who I was and embraced all of me. I never really fit into cliques or was popular. That wasn't interesting or alike because I'd stick out like a sore thumb with my difference of opinion, going my own direction. It makes much more sense now than ever. My characteristics, traits, and personality makes up the woman I am today; a woman of resilience, purpose, and distinction. To truly walk in freedom, one must embrace and accept their true identity. God has set us apart for such a time as this. We weren't meant to fit in but to stand out and be a light of the world for God's glory. We are mandated to be changed to this

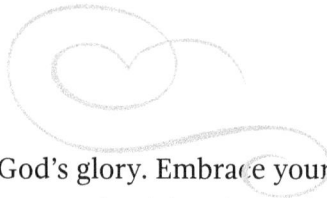

earth for God's glory. Embrace your uniqueness because you are fearful and wonderfully made. Great are God's works.

CHAPTER 18

Get Off The Sidelines

'VE ALWAYS BEEN A huge fan and cheerleader to others. I'm one of the greatest sources of encouragement and support you'd ever meet. If you sold it, I bought it. If you launched it, I helped fund it or attended it. I gave ideas and even helped brainstorm it. With every effort and drive to push another's dream, I surely can invest and put that same energy into myself. It's time to get off the sidelines and out of the shadows into birthing vision. Potential does not produce fruit. It's mere talk but no actions leading to full execution.

According to Habakkuk 2:2, "And the Lord answered me, and said, write the vision, and make it plain upon tables, that he may run that readeth it." You can write it down and make vision boards but to never follow through is insanity. Playing small leaves you focusing on short term, temporary comfort, security, relief, and validation. When you play small, you're giving up the freedom and option to live the life God truly intended, to maintain a sense of control and present security. Staying on the sidelines means our actions are motivated by fears. So what if the idea doesn't work and people don't show up? Proverbs 16:3 reads, "Commit thy works unto the Lord, and thy thoughts shall be established." God will put the right people and plans together when we include Him first.

I've learned that in life, we must take some risks to live a fulfilled life. We must take responsibility for our own happiness. Relying on someone else besides God is a recipe for a life of misery and regrets. God isn't going to present and drop everything in our laps if we won't step out on faith, and putting in work and effort. As challenges come, find strength in them, working

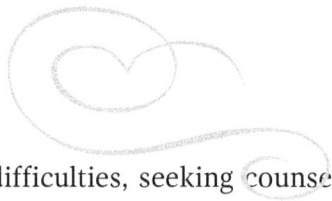

through difficulties, seeking counsel or advice, but not running away at the first sign of discomfort. Enjoy the small beginnings and wins to help catapult you to greatness.

I plan to go after everything that's mine with the strength and power of God, leaving nothing on the table. Don't be like the man at the pool of Bethesda (John 5). He watched everyone get healed as the angels came to stir the water. It wasn't until he took up his mat and walked when He received what the Lord had for him. Stop making up excuses. The season of being a lump on the log is over. Get out of the cave and go forward. Put your hands to plow and follow after God with your whole heart.

Prayers

I DECREE PHILIPPIANS 4:7, "THAT the peace of God, which transcends all understanding, will guard my heart and mind in Christ Jesus."

I rebuke the devil from speaking to me in Jesus' name.

I bind up the tormentor that will try to come against my mind in Jesus' name.

I decree that I will think thoughts that glorify the Lord.

Lord, uproot any demonic seeds in my mind.

Prayers

I plead the blood of Jesus on my mind.

I decree Romans 12:2, "That I will not be conformed to the pattern of this world, but be transformed by the renewing of my mind."

I decree 1 Corinthian 2:16, "That I have on the mind of Christ."

I decree Philippians 2:5, "That I have the same mindset as Jesus."

I decree Hebrews 8:10, "That the Word of God is in my mind and written in my heart."

I decree that I will be sober-minded.

I decree Isaiah 26:3, "That You will keep me in perfect peace because my mind stays on you."

I decree 2 Corinthians 10:5, "I cast down every high imagination that exalts itself against the knowledge of God and bring every thought captive unto the obedience of Jesus Christ."

I decree Colossians 3:2, "That I will set my mind on things above and not on earthly things."

I decree that I have a sound mind.

I decree Philippians 4:8, "That I will think on whatever is true, honest, just, pure, lovely, things of a good report, virtue, or praise."

I decree Matthew 6:22, that my eyes are healthy, full of light since it's the lamp of my body.

I decree Psalm 101:3, that I will not set anything worthless before my eyes.

Lord, open my eyes so I can behold wondrous things out of your law (Psalm 119:18).

Lord, open up my eyes so I can see what you are showing me.

Lord, turn my eyes from looking at worthless things (Psalm 119:37).

Lord, enlighten the eyes of my understanding (Ephesians 1:18).

I decree Hebrews 12:2, that I will look to Jesus, who is the author and finisher of my faith.

I decree 2 Corinthians 4:18, that I will not look to things that are seen but to the things that are unseen.

I decree Proverbs 22:9, that I have bountiful eyes and that I will be blessed.

I decree that I will not be wise in my own eyes (Isaiah 5:21).

I decree Psalm 121:1, that I will lift my eyes up to the hills from where my help comes from.

Lord, bless me to see You in the midst of the storm.

Lord, bless me to stay positive and be an encourager when things look bleak.

Lord, bless me to look at my circumstances through the eyes of faith.

Lord, remove any spiritual scales from my eyes so I can see deeper in the spirit realm.

Lord, open up my ears to hear Your still small voice.

I bind up weariness from blocking me from hearing God's voice.

I decree that I will incline my ears to hear the voice of the Lord.

I decree Proverbs 18:15 that my ears are one of the wise that seeks knowledge.

I decree Deuteronomy 29:4 that the Lord has given me a heart to know, eyes to see, and ears to hear.

I decree that I will hear what the Lord speaks and follow His commands.

I bind up my ears from being tickled by false prophecy or words from my flesh.

I decree that my ears are blessed because they hear what the Lord has spoken.

I decree Revelations 3:22 that I have an ear to hear what the Spirit of the Lord is speaking to the church.

Lord, bless my ears to be on the right frequency to always hear Your voice.

Lord, bless me to get in the right posture so I can hear Your voice.

Lord, remove any idols in my heart so I can only hear Your voice.

I decree Exodus 4:12 that God will be with my mouth and teach me what I shall say.

Lord, a good word will make my heart glad (Proverbs 12:25).

I decree Proverbs 15:23 that a man has joy by the answer of his mouth. A word spoken in due season is so good.

The Lord GOD has given me the tongue of the learned, that I should know how to speak a word in season to him that is weary (Isaiah 50:4).

I decree that I will speak positive affirmation instead of negative ones.

I decree that I will be careful of the words that I speak.

I decree that I will be slow to speak in Jesus' name.

I yield my mouth to you, Lord.

I decree that I will speak words that edify grace to the hearer.

Lord, set a guard over my mouth (Psalm 141:3).

Lord, keep the door of my lips (Psalm 141:3).

I decree Psalm 34:13 that the Lord will keep my tongue from evil and my lips from deceitful speech.

I decree Psalm 39:1 that I will watch my ways, so I don't sin with my tongue.

Lord, create in me a pure heart in Jesus' name.

Lord, you warn us that what's coming out of our mouths is an indication of what's in our hearts. Let my words bring glory to you.

Lord, you warn us that the things coming out of our mouth defile us. Bless my heart to have the right motives.

Lord, you look at my heart. I pray that I will be pleasing in your sight.

Lord, you warn us that from the heart come evil thoughts, murder,adultery, sexual immorality, theft, false testimony, and slander (Matthew 15:19; Mark 7:21). These are the reasons why I need you because You are the only One who can set me free of these wicked things.

Lord, you warn us that the good man brings good things out of the good treasures of his heart and the evil man brings evil treasures out of his heart (Luke 6:45).

Lord, make me over.

Lord, bless me to get your word deeper into my heart and never forget them so I can teach my children and grandchildren (Deuteronomy 4:9).

Lord, bless me with wisdom and guide my heart on the right course (Proverbs 23:19).

Lord, bless me not to trust in my own heart but trust in You and Your word. You warn me that he that trusts in his own heart is a fool (Proverbs 28:26).

Lord, bless me not to walk around wounded. I will cast all my cares upon you because you care for me.

Prayers

About The Author

KIMBERLY COOPER IS A native of Nesmith, South Carolina, a small rural area. Currently, she resides in Columbia, South Carolina, with her husband, Ludrick Cooper. She truly has a heart for people from every walk of life. Kimberly's passion is spreading the gospel and empowering others every chance she gets. She is serving under the leadership of ACLJ Intercontinental Ministry as an affirmed Prophet of God. Kimberly desires that all who experience hurt or trauma get the help they need. To be healed, whole, and experience restoration.

Index

C

casket, 11, 12, 28

Cervical Cancer, 18

childhood, 4, 5, 23

children, 5, 7, 9, 15, 16, 17, 73

Christ, 33, 40, 43, 51, 53, 55, 56, 58, 65, 66

Christian, 42, 43

Cierra L. Jones, 49

classmates, 4

clothes, 7, 8, 21

coat, 32, 37

Cognitive behavior therapy, 26

college, 22, 24

comfort, 11, 12, 14, 46, 63

compassion, 32, 56

conqueror, 51

conversation, 30, 45

cousin, 11

covenant, 60

culture, 29

D

dad, 10, 17, 22, 23, 30

O

P

www.ingramcontent.com/pod-product-compliance
Lightning Source LLC
Chambersburg PA
CBHW070539030426
42337CB00016B/2275